PATRICIA BRODY
Dangerous To Know

salmonpoetry

Published in 2013 by
Salmon Poetry
Cliffs of Moher, County Clare, Ireland
Website: www.salmonpoetry.com
Email: info@salmonpoetry.com

ISBN 978-1-908836-21-2

COVER ARTWORK: *'Lyre' by Tom Kostro – www.behance.net/tomkostro*
COVER DESIGN: *Siobhán Hutson*

Printed in Ireland by Sprint Print

The book in your hands is for the women in it.

Lost through their sex and through the ages, I found them through their male shields, their voices disguised: John's wife Anne Donne; William's sister, Dorothy Wordsworth, Orazio's daughter Artemisia Gentileschi, Byron's "groupie" Lady Caroline Lamb.

The title is taken from Lamb's excited diary entry after first meeting Lord Byron: "Mad, bad and dangerous to know."

But she was talking about herself.

My mother, cool blond from the frozen fifties, wrote and erased her poems, my Russian-born grandmother, murdered in her Nova Scotia kitchen, for becoming "too outspoken." And for making money.

I write these women's stories here to rouse them from 100 or 1000 years of restless death. As every goddess knows, nothing's worse than being ignored.

Patricia Brody

For My Family
I never writ, without TK and our three: Z, K, C

I read *Glenarvon* too by Caro Lamb.
God damn.
BYRON

My verses — mine.
CARO LAMB

Contents

I.

II.

III.

I.

WHEN YOU MEET HER

Enter her sun–washed studio.
        Behind the drape of silk,
her outrage. Her affair with color.

                ★

Not as other lady painters of the day
        who hide in still-life.

                ★

She is the figure in blue.

AMERICAN GIRL, July 5th

Here in filtered light
summer begins.
Supper outside almost done, warm air
slips an arm around her bare shoulders:
You could grow young again.
Towards seven she stands at the edge
of a golf course, watching
three young players, arrogant
with health,   their chests stretch
their clingy polo shirts. Laughing
they strut their game away,
knocking off those charged *zaps*,
tap, *smack* – who cares
where that ball goes –
where, a generation before
on that rolling green, she let
him kiss her in the dark –
his roughness at sixteen.
She remembers his hoarse voice,
the anger in it, when he said,
"I'm gonna kiss you *right*."

THE SHINY GIRL

She bobs in the ocean
her long hair, her olive shoulders, the water
olive too, deeper by a thousand shades
holds her legs, sluices her neck
the tawny girl who turns to me and smiles
        and turns

Lolling and rising
teasing the breast of the sea
silver and blue in the sea
her suit a wire-shock of blue
piercing the shock of the wave

She surfaces   and smiles
        and turns
in the late sun, when the gulls return
to claim what they've left behind
(to claim the girl from me?)
the shiny girl in the sea

I stand at the edge,   holding her towel.

ARCHEOLOGY

My husband confessed

he found the jawbone
of my mother's Maine Coon.
Tarzan.

$\star$

Each loss −
− *the crumbling*
of a small civilization.

$\star$

Tarzan's small grave
− he was young −
hastily scraped //
in the lower corner of the backyard.

$\star$

Mother piled stones.
The house's one-third acre is its emerald
          the plot so brightly green
the grass −

$\star$

Siblings & pets twine their voices
with gnarled roses & the apple tree
glistening
on summer mornings

$\star$

robin reds & jay-screech blues
praising & pecking the rickety garden
& the white blossoms.

       Beneath that tree each sister wed
leaves a-quiver & words a-choir

green as when the world was fire
           Not to mention I'd buried

     ★

two hamsters & a baby turtle named
Tom-thumb. I was six with dad

in his overcoat,   just off the train
the ground frozen, pale, under a grey snow
       & spring mocking.

     ★

I screamed when I thought I saw
    the body stir
        furry & wind-whipped

in daddy's palm
the smallest possession
       I loved & feared its dying
would shatter my house.

     ★

First, my husband said
there was a patch of fur & the skull
the next day only the jawbone.

★

Mother stood at the back door
in her pink robe.

She called out instructions
from a distance
we were freezing
Father's patience   or penitence
kept us going

       He brought it home, my husband
The papery fragment of bone (telling no one)
thinking to clean it

       ★

preserve it like a stone.
But it was too delicate
the remains of mother's reckless kitten
& crumbled
       like a small civilization.

GLUHWEIN

Trample on a doormat or a rose.
You *clump clump* o'er the ornery road
in your mail-order Alpen,   romance green,
your clogs the clumpy croak of a toad.

I don't know why we order such shoes!
It's enough to make the mailman curse & moan
or break into Tyrolean white-blues.
Once I walked with my love, god

we were young.   God he was not.
Though when you are that greeny age, whom
you love – quick (as in some poems)becomes
your slickest deity. Clip-clop.

We walked on blank white ribbons in the snow.
Skeletons of trees clocked the trail.
He wore black & I wore black, fur trimmed.
Fur around the frosty face and tail.

(In the Alps, beasts of prey lurk lightly.)
The best part of the hike was when we fell
off the shuffly path – – *Crunch!   Pell mell*
tromping to a Gasthaus, low & sweet.

Through the dumpling   through the warm door
the minstrel at the bench *zinging* lieder.
Ach your cold ears!   *Ach* the zither!
The dirndl lady leads us to our table.

In dialect, my beaux, call them Rudi,
order fleshy essence, apple strudel.
Pulling off wet wool, freeing fingers.
Enter the white pitcher, steaming, creamy.

Wine floats up as breath.　Cloves.　It's *Gluhwein.*
Glow cloaks our tongues, stings our lips.
Simmering with eidelweiss, it whispers:
Yodl-ay-ee-oo, Love me do.

TWIST on TRYST

Great love of my loves
who taught me loss and fire
                    O Flame of flames
has taken to calling on my mother.

Old sweet sin, who lives nearby. True
        I asked him to, but
                    I was just testing.

True, we haven't kindled
        the candle for decades
                    except the occasional funeral

our wet eyes a-clamor
        like Donne's violets
                    on the bank of the river. . .

He humors her humors
repairs a white fence

re-hinges a storm door

not that bad-boy I longed for   but

he's courting her approval.
O light of my young nights   *He's not calling me*
honey man I did adore and she
                    abhorred.   I used to slide under

the lilied bubbles   and imagine him in the water   Oh
I'd say, not breathing in
Oh

DISORGANIZED

The usual frenzy.
She's supposed to perform, tonight.
But nothing's right from top to toes.
She's brought the wrong clothes.

She's meant to sing, tonight.
Whooh, that hair, cropped too close.
She's brought the wrong clothes
and her face looks pasty.

Awful hair, cropped too close.
Maybe if she tries again? Nope, too frizzy.
With her pasty face −   − even worse.
The roots covered but at what cost.

She tries again: Where's her real hair?
Feet bare.
Roots covered but petals lost.
She looks absurd − the fat girl curse.

Feet bare,   no dress, there's the bell!
                         oh god, they'll talk −
she's sweating in another borrowed robe.
Absurd, short-sleeved , too tight to close.
Well, too bad. Let them gawk!

Wearing yet another borrowed robe
she's forced to sing her number in the tub.
Well, let them gawk.
Vapors rise as she sings, *Haven't you noticed − −*

She's forced to sing in the tub
sometimes on pitch.
Vapors rise, *Suddenly bright and breezy − −*

But if she belts, can she sustain — the rush
                                    — the harmony?

In the bath, on pitch
the well-dressed orchestra finds her.
She belts — — the rush! The harmony.

She raises her arm through leafy-steam.

The orchestra joins her, crooking their fingers
                    You are precisely...my cup of tea
through leafy steam, she hears her voice
rise like violins, her voice

My cup of tea, so what
if she's not dressed, her violins
rise like vapor to the rafters.
She holds her note and hears   the breeze

her violins
undress
right from their tops to their toes.
The usual frenzy, the song.

YOU GO RIDING WITH THE FAMOUS EDITOR

You go
        the old way : on horseback
over reservoir and rill.
Imagine following that domed head   *Galloping galloping*
through daisy-dotted field
past sun-bathed joggers and mallards.
You've hired your velvet ponies
from the city's last stable   Claremont
to flick the crop and breathe the oats   urban squires
                        seeking a whiff of the old hunt.

The wild flight through the trees.

The horses whinny and shy
                off the path sharply
to guzzle buttercups
                out of your control
Oh the glow   the man and you in Nature.
Miles away from fumes and bus
though you can't be alone, naturally
the Professor and you.
To think you've got him almost to yourself
not a stressed syllable in sight − − except
except,   there's always a rival, more dazzling
younger, boyish,
it's never clear
you haven't a clue   where he's leading − −
at least you have this sun-drenched hour *Galloping galloping*
hope you won't be put to pasture
        yet,   you *feel* positive,   positively pastoral
this golden-gaited Gotham morn.
Pastor Olmsted's   rocks and falls   gentle swells
sweet Central, like a green thought:

                    Who is this courtly fellow
you court with word-caresses
praying he'll reward you   page you. . .   Dare you
hand him a letter?   Will he call you later?
Whoa, there. Time to return the horses.

ALTHEA'S GAME

Mother named me goddess, long-limbed.
My hair   the night let down
loose from its Gibson knot,   spilling
past shoulders   to cover bare arms.
Mulberry lips   dusky skin

limbs quick and light   as if I leapt
colors spilling
                from an Isadora dawn.
I didn't laugh or wink.   My long swing
broke the barrier for Venus & Serena.
The *Times* suggested my life

lacked something.
Leaving — as the *Times* must
the life
spilled.   I slammed that ball
straight to the mulberry sun.

Look with awe.
River of hair,   river of white dress,
berry-lips pressed down.
Watch me spill
my   self   into the sun's waiting arms.
Long   shimmer   on   grass.

Such delicacy. Iron limbs,
the *p-l-o-ck!* of catgut on wool-skin,
the crowd's gasp.
My shadow leaps, my stroke is black
                                    lightning,
long.
How do I not die?

II.

SALAD NIGHTS

Over the oil & vinegar
she sits beside me,   nothing acknowledged
though I know
she likes to eat together
while we may   this blossom
I watered until she grew into petals
that blaze in spring.
                    She's added
dried cranberries, walnuts, slices
of Mutsu,   Golden Delicious — potions
she gets from some goddess,
vine-wreathed,   grape juice sticky
on her lips. For the dressing
we squeeze splashes of orange, lime.
Is it because today
I visited the crotchety OB
who first handed her to me
I say, I remember giving birth.   *Ew*
she says.   The labor was long.
He bade me rise
off the birthing chair where
I crouched like a beggar.
With his staff he broke the water.
Then she was ready, tidal swimmer,
in the curl, in the girl, I knew.
                Out she wriggled   ripped   dripping
                ripe with the dawn & dew.

THE FRUIT-LIFE OF MOTHERS

The voluptuous bowl held us all.
Told us we had plenty, would be full,
contained, that we   could

put our teeth
to the chalky skin of Bartletts,
the silk of plums,

and pierce and suck the juice,
and tongue the yielding meat.
Winter, the green pyrex bowl

gleamed on the counter,
golden Boscs, red-glint Macouns.
Mother got advice from

Mr. Murdoch's column,
Season Picks. She acquired
country wisdom the longer she languished

in the land of farm-stands.
Summer sparkled in the cool
cave, the bowl's

ripe offer chilled
your palm, the only part soft enough to hold
such round, helpless

jewels: drunk juice-balloons.
Baby-lush flesh, tumbled
nectarines, melons, cherries.

We had a common mission she and I,
the search for the perfect peach.
My life is half over.

BLOODY LULLABY
(Brahms' *Wiegenlied,* Op. 49)

Lullaby
     We carried her,
     curled starfish
and goodnight
     from thought ember
     to somber embryo
bright angels
     who peered through
     the womb's bell shadows.
watch o'er thee
     I inched my steps,
     not one false move
Lullaby
     to keep our pretty swimmer
     safe within.
and goodnight
     From spark
     to lit star:
thy mother's delight
     We made our child.

     Now, the doctor cocks his eye:
Lay thee down
     pulls her soft arm straight,
     struggles for the tiny vein
now and rest
     draws cherry blood
     into his tube.
May thy slumber
    Her bewildered cry
    is the rest.
be blest

THE REFUSAL

Our firstborn will not eat.
Blue-white and withered to a wraith, isn't he
lording it over us, the little prince
of pain?

Our downy boy knows how to play
his mother like a fiddle:
he cries on a dime,
crinkles up his eyes,
plies us with his grin,
or sits there with his fork
scraping his death wish
across his dinner plate
                    not eating, not eating.

The little beak
we built a life around
is making sounds of dying.

How would you handle your bone child,
the boy you waited for?

You paced the floor,
your brand-new bundle, sleepless,
– all he wanted was your breast –
held him close, half the night
until the monsters left. . .
and led him off to school,
neither one of you bearing
ever to let go.

STOPPING BY 106TH
& BROADWAY

It is snowing on the synagogue across the street.
It is snowing on the mourners, swaying in the snow.
It is snowing on the deli, the sliced meat.
It is snowing on the lamppost with its other-century glow.
It is snowing on Memory, her dress, her slender feet
      jeweled in the first thin frost of snow.
It is snowing on Straus Park, the lost Titanic story:
      earth reaps the bones of Ida and Isador
      lost at sea
      (*lovely and pleasant were they in their lives*
      and in their death they were not divided)
      clasping − merged − in their song-filled sleep.
It is snowing on Memory, her icy feet.
It is snowing on the moth-wing scorched last July.
It is snowing on the oranges and pears left for Memory
      to wear as an offering, awkward, sweet.
It is snowing on my father.

KENNEBEC

Wake, the morning brims
her sky plum-streaked with vestiges of sleep.

Blue heron splash-skims the river glass
seeking shimmer-bite fish.

Our children dream through this.
White terns, ravenous cormorants

double-banded plover.
Coffee musk silver hour.   Rise
                                    mother.

THE COURTSHIP

He meandered Florentine alleys
scrounging their one-moan honeymoon.
She recounts, "We fought the whole time over
Forever Amber."
No Della Robbia for him,
no robin's egg
Madonna col bambino –

Remember as a kid when
you first realized *They did it?*

Do he and I connect?
What mission, closer
and closer until –
Eureka!   The new me. And we mosey
on up the road, those white star-shaped
blooms burst into fragrance.
He sees a cardinal, the bird he loves best –
of course this never happened,
Daddy and his baby girl,
our mercurial joining,
one quick and lovely blink
and down I tumble down
        the slope behind him.

"He never learned to swim properly,"
mother would complain. "He doesn't use his legs."
I saw him thrust through grey churn, shouting,
This'll wake you up!
Once he saved my sister from an undertow in Mexico.

Everything will remind me.

WE WERE DEAD

We were dead, we were leaping over snow.
That's where I thought I'd find you
plowing through fresh-noon drift on the old slope.
You had just departed.
I heard your breath in the cold space
                                                between birches.
Crisp, tingling −   happy?   You blow out
you breathe in.   You blow out

the breath-cloud's little mockery of ghost.
 − −   I cried your first name into the blue.
Noon-sun, hot-cold   as when   you'd force me to come out,
leave my cheese & mac, my book,   *Lad, a Dog.*
Creamy bite, then zip the parka
                                        tumble out in snow.
Sister's winter pasture.   I climb until I reach the altar.
Crotch of poplar   polar ghostly bells.

Last summer's shivering , O silver bells.
Unzip the down,   lean through
& whisper your code to the chasm / *your name*
Surely you'd come out if you were
                                        anywhere
Tree, you'd say, spicing the syllable /   my name
That peppery murmur   *my dotter*
So we'll be dead together, snowy father.

DADDY'S DISH

I served him a saucer of just-rinsed blue,
gnarled old critter – waking for food –
he hunkered down over his plate of fruit
lapping and crunching through puckery skins
till he reached childhood's tart tongue   (where pleasure = sin).
"These were the berries grew best in Glace Bay,"
his mother simmering syrupy pans,
purple jam for the one sweet lick in their
dour winter.
      So I brought him a scoop of vanilla,
the thrill so deep sent shivers down his spine.
"Now *this* is a meal,"   familiarly intoned,
his leaky, lovely heart (in spite of her, or *her*, or me)
                              set pining
for his bitter-blue, only kind of home.

AMERICAN DESIRE, July 3

You want to commune with someone hot as July.
You want to lie
right on top
New York City's   black-edged peaks
                              arching over you   the sun
spiking
the clouds' swollen bellies.
They are lit from within: Explosive −
                              primed for the festivities
soon to come.
                    To come, bursts   broken cries
then the long, dangling spray of
                                     colored lights.
Stella's lights.
Firecracker *RED   BLUE   WHITE*
                      Now, breathe − −   that he would
set his hand
on your waist,   your vital / most vital −
& you'll shift   ever so slightly   at the *bang!*
And the sky will fall.

ABLAZE IN SIBERIA (Irises)

Today at their peak of violet youth
their moist blooms hang open.
Purple wattles droop.
Pouty lips invite who may come.

>Before climbing to the x-ray table
>I read: **Bones At Peak Density From 25–35**.
>After that we lose, lose, lose until
>bones so thin, we snap.

Two pale dancers – *mariposas* –
rise like veils above the fluttering purple.

>*Bz-z-z-z!* The x-ray's cranky groan
>nicks my hip, wrist, spine
>my legs part as she tells me
>*Use the metal V.*
>How insistently she avoids my eyes!
>*Click-click, click-click* her fingers tap
>clearly, she is tired of measuring
>the bird-bones. Austere in her adherence
>to one vocal tone:
>*The report will be sent to your doctor.*
>Outside this door, stacked in sample-packs
>every pill known to woman. A fix
>for every orifice and organ.

You could cup your hand under the tallest blossom
peer down the dark-veined flower-throat
turn up the corners of your own flesh-mouth

as if trying   to match markings   with *their*
yellow-wisped,   plum-striped wings.
Deep in the iris-cup you could probe,   each center petal-tip
poised   –   gazing out from *in*
like the painted geisha-eye   on a butterfly.

III.

UNDONNE

"John Donne, Anne Donne, Undone"

> — JOHN DONNE's note to his 17-year-old wife
> upon his imprisonment for their secret marriage.

After they hauled you off to jail,
    leaving me the ruined bed
    the cramps
the moist ache there,

I staggered in cold air
    frail vine stripped   you, the "abler" stalk.
    Vainly I twist toward Sunrise.

Morning-after: rosy petals blown,
    hearts,   wine-stained bedclothes,   strewn.
    And where's that *busy fool*

who should have roused us   –   where, this dawn?
    No warning beam.   Instead of breakfast
    courtyard shouts   boot-stomp   jay-caw
rend   our first unribboned rising.

We dreamed like babes   milk-ravished,
    eyes closed,   but close betrothed.
    Mark this bruise,   you breathed, purple beneath

my torn shift.   My throat,   my breast,   used.
    Just hours ago your tongue formed
all the words I knew.

Love's quick sup   –   now done?
    Courtier,   your wit
    streaks through me. So they

banish you, for lack of fee.   Father!
      You'd dress me in weeds?   None
      come to comfort your sapling-bride;
my door shamed,   my love-bed early graved.

Don't leave me here!
      (The day warms.)   Again . . .   last kiss.
I turn from your sudden vanishing.

WILLIAM'S SHY ROMANTIC

She breathed her own ethers into his words.
Recorded pine, cloud-cave, brother's footfall,
felt fog stir, heard lightning release, denied
her own bruised feet, wrenched spine, rent heart
with the starched nightdress, under the pillow.
Brewed late-day, spiked possets, cooled his hot head.
Too soon, he brought Mary and seven babes.
She nursed them too with mother-herbs,
chamomile, the poppies and packed journal
tossed out in her green world to curl yellow.
She anticipated, enflamed his muse.
                    Well, what was she to do? She did for two.
If he were mouthpiece, even brain,
she was lute, reflex let-down, milk-blue rain.

DANGEROUS TO KNOW

"Mad, bad, and dangerous to know"

LADY CAROLINE LAMB's journal entry,
on first meeting Lord Byron, 1812

I've been chilling with these dead people,
        not just reading their letters and poems
but going to their balls.

I've been under their clothes
        in their skins,
sticking to dampened petticoats

and floaty muslin.
        I'm at Devonshire House;
Lady Someone is my mother.

At Brocket I'm running through the trees,
        a lordly satyr at my heels, his lip
curled, his brow furred, pale skin agleam,

his hair black as the moors, of course.
        "I know not," I say in some confusion
"but this I believe; the hand of heaven never

impressed on man a countenance
        so beautiful..." oh
if it falls on me −

There are parties and morning calls,
        dances from Allemagne and Spain
swirling the halls. These *most nervous* affairs!

Fly me, says the mad corsair.
        Deep-drugged in the night
I creep from bed, Lord M stretched

senseless beside me.
        Down through Georgiana's garden
I fall, down to the white hawthorn

as the mist rises from wet petals
        and opium swells in syrupy draughts,
I swoon: For God's sake! Sherry!

(Sips from Spain revive me.)
        And the susurrous leaves will
waken the heat in my reborn thighs.

Over the moonstones I leap, snapping twigs.
        Grass clings to my winged soles.
"Do you know what I've done?" sneers he.

"I've heard but I know it is false," I breathe.
        "No, I've done what they say," he boasts.
How can I not cry out?

He reaches to crush me into his coat,
        his thigh strums through my gown,
I drink his sighs in the moonlight –

broken gasps – *Greek and natural*;
        we are so gone, we are so pale,
and his maimed foot throbs in the soil.

SISTERS & MASTERS

When he called Dorothy to *come and bring no book*,
when maids go Maying green-gowned, wreathed in whitethorn,
do they replay,   renew,   reveal,   revamp   some
lush Druid legend?

Dryad w/dragon, virgin w/satyr, flame-
horse w/master, brother w/sister, no
eye on danger. Danger! Dorothy's gone milking;
What was he asking?

When he called from breakfast, *Come*, hurry, hurry,
she, so ordered and concealing, no one's sweet-
meat, dropped her rose-stained glove, journal-leaves blazed up.
Wild-fire girl gauzed in

wildflowers. No bridal blindfold, world-upside-
down, but sees Corinna trip through dawn May-glazed,
gone, fling herself fragrantly on grass.
                              How that
glittering takes her.

MID-LEAP

To purify I must first soften
LETITIA ELIZABETH LANDON

Days before the "poisoning" she wrote
(This Sappho hounded all the way to Ghana}
of the breeze under the yum-yum trees
cheerful letters back to London   "home."
Mr. Maclean, her bridegroom, took care of the rest.
What   of her   remains
                                in the sands   at Castle Coast.
She kept falling

and falling.   The lovebird in her low-cut gown.
I mean the girl couldn't win. Too sexy
for her clothes, her pose too harsh for husbands,
too ditzy for women's lib.   Simp   Victim
Flirt.   Beauty-truth/ truth – –
too loose, too quick
the rumors flew,   they'd say,   her work
"By Byron out of LEL"   As if she were brood mare
as if there were a child.
                          Except this sea-swept isle,
                          this chorus of smoke and lyre.

Even Disraeli dropped his *mot*:
"Snub-nosed Sappho."
Her logo,   her body-palindrome:
                          Logic – Ethics – Lays
                          Lily –   Escape –   Lily –
How could she say,   which Sappho

which *autho-real* shout   Rose from her throat
                          with her perfumed breath
Which wind in the rose-wreathed hair…
Or whose form, *outlined on the sunny air.*

47

TELL ME ONE THING IF YOU CAN

from *The Letters of Abelard and Heloise, c. 1120*

1.
His handmaid, or rather daughter, wife, or rather sister

Yes, she speaks, despite the throng at Père Lachaise,
despite her weepings and lamentations.

His Magdalene-martyr, nailed on her cross d'amour
after her *master, or rather father, husband, or rather brother*

covers her in convent, throws a burqa over
her bruised mouth, still clamoring for his.

He's schooled her, pumped her
full of Abelardian jizz —

Look, he's wrenched her from
floral virgin to fruited vixen

fanned her girded loins
plumbed her mind and womb

then dropped her cold   with no comfort
not a powdered ram's horn   or reeking poultice

to soothe those libidinal quakes
not even her *baby* —   Astrolabe —   the plum

of those heretic minglings,   who might
divert her from love's madness:

the wet-lipped visits during Mass,
the hot-tongued whimpers at Vespers,

the writhings and contortions   beneath
her habit,   to hide Satan's flames.

O ultimate Husband!   O unworthy
of my marriage bed —   Why

did I marry you?   Now take
your excoriated flesh!   I, Abbess

must also burn,   singing your most
personal,   delicious hymn.

      2.
Tell me I say or I will tell the world what I think.

Even a sip of wine at supper
was to   summon *lewd pleasures*

He had of course inhaled me in the studio

afternoon sun beat through the drapes   blind heat
soaked skin   nothing was enough

     his mouth drew kisses *from my soul's abyss*

At noon   I bathe the scourged   "parts in shame"
in balm of white narcissus,   lemon-thyme

dawn-pressed from the neighbor's vineyard
grape-must   cognac
the draw of purple fire on the tongue

3.

I spend my day   with hymns you sent,
Evensong.   How is it you quote Sappho
sign   her sea and moss ?   She calls me   *Abbess*

dawn wets the grass   the breeze
wafts its fragrance to my airless cell –
Time to scour the kitchen   my women
call for bread and milk

O gauze above the Seine
O cloth of stars
This old habit.

SHE FALLS FOR CURE
After LEL

So, she dumps her first love,
drunk on wine-dark
the kind that burns
　　　　　her poet brain.

Fame, like sunlight,
dazzles her ascent.
Eyes that never saw mine　　*yet slept with me.*

Such is the power of that liquid lyre.
−　Love's low notes −
roses　　　　　swans

their necks　　　at long length

Words that died in utterance.

First love?　　First chill.
Still −　　its　incense　　clings
when her new drug dances in …　　Yes,

Youth.　　Same bedroom eyes −　　It's him.　　It's　Phaon.
When he speaks her heart beats　quicker　　& the light − −
But.　　　　He trumps her　——　& worse, forgets

she is who she is −　　famous, adored,
Love's　troubadour −
You think she'd learn:

51

There's just no cure.   Last sweep
                                of the lyre
& up. . . up Aeolia's slope   her hair
her   wave-whipped dress   sheered
                                by salt.

How lightly she steps off

The BYRONIC BED

She sent him a lock of her pubic hair with a note signed
"Your Wild Antelope."

Here I am tonight and every night
bedding Lord Byron
in the guise of a calmer Caroline.
Did I say calm? Whirling dervish, devilish
poet-stalker − −   only the disease, her fluent
       body flooded,
toxic fluid − −   only the dropsy stopped her.

She and her all-night balls, her scandal-novels, her
final fall.   She crooned through the night
"ill-fated rose,"   the river Elle gurgled, flooding
out the lines she bawled for Byron
who withdrew. . . "until we two are chained by the Devil
together in Dante's Inferno,"   and again flew
        to her −   Caroline

helpless as a moon-crazed moth: *Caro*
your poor heart − *what a volcano,* her
heart, he said, pumped lava, her blood the Devil's
heat, for him.
           The stroke of midnight:
they meet by the lake, swans a-shimmer, His
clubfoot heavy in the grass, her pale face flooded.

For once his smirk relaxes; her cooing drowned, this blood-
wine, left in the glass.   *Caroline*
Lamb silenced?   Byron's
vanity − the bitch they loved to hate, her
boy-slim form bloated.   *Serves her right*
they said, yet were aghast, even she should come to this.
        The Devil

must have wooed her, the poet, the devil-
poet. She couldn't stop — trinkets, love-notes, brawls — flaunting
the locks from private places,   the nights
exploded: cross-dressing, fake pregnancy, carried
past term.   He read the *Childe* to her, his hand cupped her
trembling breast, she drank his latest cup —   Byron!

London's glorious boy, hers for the demon-hour — he
detested her "feverish dream" but she deviled

his steps. *Remember thee!* — he spat. She sued, her
last gasps tear the over-flooded
page. "That angel. . . "   Caroline
dying: *I loved him past shame, I still love* —   this night

never ends —   you red-lipped Lord. Devils
make the best lovers. Her cries flood
my pillow. Lady C and Lord B,   tonight.

In SHELLEY'S 'LOVE'S PHILOSOPHY' THE RHYME IS SLANT

Let's zoom in on that high heart
(poet pouting for a kiss?) drowned
                              then burnt
while Byron stood by
burned too.   But he could swim
Byron   much tormented by the scene:
his soul-mate washed up on the beach
at Viareggio   the body doused with oil and wine − then
lit
the rival-soul left   upright, but hobbled   hating it.

Shelley gave them noms de plume
Julian and Maddalo.
                    And plumed they were, the two
ladies' men   worth kissing.   Men lost
to the sea, to love's crossings.

river/forever   heaven/forgiven   kiss/kiss not

DRESSED AS A BOY

Because of his clubfoot, Byron would not waltz.

I glide   through his locked door.
    This is how he liked me best,
        my limbs packed in tight breeches.

Don't try to resist me   rising
    in Ariel's winged slippers
        to those lips − he holds me there − as if we dance.

His fingers flex, to rip
    the jabot at my throat, the same cream-silk
        he wore. He sat out,

was obsessed
    and *would* not − waltz − *waltz voluptuous*
                    bodies flung,
    the wantonness − who wouldn't rather *fly*?

Impatiently I tap my glittering toe,
    scoring each leap   poet-fawn to Regent foe,   sliding
        one... to William, my adoring Lamb. And back

two . . . my Lord Lyrical − I in*hale* his fame −
who would not —
    sway with me, but begged me quit, to lean on him

briefly. What he craved were my "connexions."
    Fool for blood, he flutters in my ear,
        Just *trust* *my* *rhyme, Caro.*

Harrow-schoolboy talk   soaked in other ladies'
    moony light. Curse this night.   I toss the *copies*
        of his love notes into my bonfire. . . Ooo-la, "the *lava*."

I burn in three-step time, still dying
    for him to dance.
        Still dying for him to stop me.

OH EARLY MODERN

What graves: Heloise with her mister at Père Lachaise,
Margaret, less undressed, well-wedged beneath Westminster
(where even Byron was forbidden).
Oh lady seers/ how bold thy tracks. Your outcries your laments,
　　your Latin & your
science, there's not a patch of grind. Take your places,
waft your wisdom. All you wished for hovers.
Fragrance, river, synapse, *your* energy lifts you from humus to vapor,
you get the full sky-swim; you get the arc.
Two robed refulgences. Heloise exhorts, Margaret brays, their wit
amazes in the Book of Days: Heloise black, meek nun's pose,
Margaret velvet, atomic headgear, matching hose.
　　　　　　　　They called her mad, but Heloise they didn't call.
Her "seducer," *he* was called, *come to the window*
oh unhorned putrefaction. What waggle will you now?
You call yourself unique, Eunuch? Never doubt, the blood
dries, but the wound's livid.
What will you do, knock her up and bolt the key? (He wrote songs!)
　　Baby's in the casement
　　mixing up the raiment
Hel, the mother, prepares evening makeovers: *chism? clism?*
What will she / will we/ next pray? Compose him-less hymn,
break holy bread, as well thy comely leg, Sisters moony.
Slouch toward homecoming, soul-queen duet:
Twice lovely, fresh-as-morn, hey-nonny-day!
Right *Blazing World,* so green we met.

NOTE: The Description of a New World, Called The Blazing-World, 1666
Fantasy-Science Fiction, by Margaret Cavendish, Duchess of Newcastle—
mocked in 17th c. Britain as "Mad Madge" later praised by Virginia Woolf and
21st c. feminists.

THROUGH A KEYHOLE DARKLY

They had on bathrobes.
Actually he never wore a robe.
She did,   white satin,
radiant with what I didn't know.
The joy of her own beauty,   or just sex.
Her bleach-blonde gleamed like the Breck girl's.
As if she were a bride.
She did look wholesome,
wouldn't wear frills.
She was a kind of boy-mom.
Strong arms for baseball, not for oatmeal.
Her skin, bronze
her lipstick Hot Coral, and she smoked.

They used to drink coffee with dinner.
Then a cigarette, between bickers.
He wouldn't waste a new one.
Instead, he'd pick up butts,
pinch them in his broad-tipped fingers.
When he puffed, he did: short, forceful pulls
like a rebel-teen, kissing.
What if he burned his tongue?
For her the smoke was velvet,
snaky, pale.
She must have melted for that
                          fine inhale.

WHEN YOU MEET ART

Enter her sun-washed studio.
Behind the drape of yellow silk
her outrage.   Her affair with color.

★

Judith Slaying Holofernes

Rivulets of blood run down the clean sheets.
How the light catches the folds.
        The difficulty of holding down a struggling general
as she saws through bone & sinew.

The figure in blue is Judith.

Judith.   Esther, before Ahasueras.
She pounds her own features into her pigments.
Not as other lady-painters of the day
        who hide in still-life and portraits.

★

Artemisia is Ambitious

She rages against her rapist
against all would-be rapists
against her helpless father
        helpless self
What you tell me I cannot, I can

★

She Paints Sound

Judith & her maid Abra
stuff Holofernes' bloody head into a sack.
Whsst!　　I hear a noise!

The mistress Judith holds up her hand
throwing a purple shadow-pool
across her face to shield
from the dazzling light.

Sleeves rolled up, she hacks off Holofernes' head.
Her other hand clenches her sword.

She & Abra —
　　　In their lavish silk
working together.

★

Maddalena

Longed for the feel
of his helpless broken feet
silked in her warm hair.
Her lids heavy
her lips thick & soft
she nods in the chair, fingers in her hair.

Mary-Maria who washed the weary feet
then dried him with her sweet gold hair.
Then dreamed of it.

She gazes in her mirror.　　Her eyes dilate.
　　　She will change everything.
Her gorgeous dress, the glow.

In the mirror her dress
           falls from one shoulder.
The burnish of the hair
caught in flame.

                                    Floating

from the shell-curve of her ear
the most opulent pearl.

Her eyes widen in fear.
The glass reflects her shimmer.
She will repent.

In the bronze, sun-drenched night
Yes, in Italy even the shadows glow yellow. . .

            ★

Artist as Prostitute

Woman anoints herself
Tuscan yellow − − yellow silk.

Feminist critics find these paintings lacking in 'feminist expression.'

The yellow robe keeps falling.
          To lure the viewer
          as it did the elders?

          To show the Carravaggi-esque
of women's disarray?   Or because we are uneven
wearing our asymmetry as a dress.

            ★

Show us our asymmetry.
　　　The burdened shoulder
　　　& the bare flesh.
Care & loss of it.
Innocence & that instant
of silk.

NOTE: Titles of paintings and quotations from Orazio and Artemisia Gentileschi: Father and Daughter Painters in Baroque Italy (Metropolitan Museum New York City, Audio Tour by Keith Christiansen, Judith W. Mann, 2001)

NO AFTERLIFE

What's Blooming

White wood aster
Elderberry, soothes labor
And of course, Touch-me-not.
Do touch me.

★

Dinosaur-Egg Plums Now in Season

Who will know reading this, such plums
as these, heads that roll, full of thought,
mouthing psalms.

★

History

My Grandmother, who lived on 5th
Had her feet done weekly by a woman named Belle.
Offering to do my toes, Belle said,
"My polish covers a multitude of sins."

★

Death

Those men in Karachi, lured.   Be   headed
Pearly-throated dad to be, hair of black and luster,
lustrous and lovely jaw!
The smoldering type – the Jew.
And what about the mother?
This isn't poetry, isn't poetry   at *those two Red Seas freely ranne*

> One from the Trunke, another from the Head
> His eyes will twinckle, and his tongue will roll
> As though he beckend, cal'd backe his soule...

★

O throat, O head.
Rod Stewart got throat cancer,
Freud, jaw.
Those cigars. Father said,
Cancer is madness.
Denied.

★

Don JUan
Tis sad to hack into the root of things.

★

If You Have a Baby

Oh my melon-colicky baby.
He wouldn't stop no matter what I did.
Breast, bubble, change, sing.
We used to put on head phones,
blast the Rolling Stones/ the Boss/
and Bruce would squall
and he would squall,
                    Rockabye, rockabye.
BORN in the USA!

★

Byron's Contraries

(to his Banker)

Was he never in a Turkish bath
    That marble paradise of sherbet and sodomy?

            (to his Publisher)
You have so many divine poems,
    Is it nothing to have written a Human one?

            ★

O CANADA!

At Seymour Place where you, Doc, see no more,
You used to sing a few bars —
& mama banged the ivories, *I'm in the mood for love…*

"Winter's here yet!" you'd yell.
How you groaned and groveled as you fell.
We had to bury you —

            ★

Byron's Last

Delirious in Greece he begged,
    Don't let the docs hack the body!
    Most of all: *Can* the leeches!
Did they listen?
Well, they did keep the brain in a jar.

            ★

The Waltz

    They're selling postcards of the hanging: Elizabethan fixation
        on ribald word-play : Death and the sexual spasm.

Still dying for him to dance.

★

Crossing the Channel

Esp: Delacroix re: Byron

That hand! The silk sleeve falls back
like a woman's robe, his inner wrist bared.
The pallor he poured upon my skin —
As if death could   —   the moonlit arm
reaching from the ruined rocks
                                        of Missolonghi.

Acknowledgements

Grateful acknowledgment to publications where these poems, some in earlier versions, appeared:

Barrow Street: "Oh Early Modern"
BigCity Lit: "The Byronic Bed," "Tell Me One Thing If You Can" as "Heloise to Her Castrato"
Diner: "Undonne"
International Feminist Journal of Politics: "Kennebec"
Junctures (NZ): We Were Dead
The Paris Review and *Chance of a Ghost* (anthology): "Dangerous to Know"
Poet Lore: "Stopping By 106th & Broadway"
Psychoanalytic Perspectives: "The Refusal"
Red Mountain Review: "The Fruit-life of Mothers"
Room of One's Own (Canada): "American Girl, July 5th"
The Same: "Althea's Game"
Vallum (Montreal): "Bloody Lullaby"
Western Humanities Review: "William's Shy Romantic," "Sisters & Masters," "In Shelley's 'Love's Philosophy' the Rhyme is Slant," "You Go Riding with the Famous Editor"

Some of the poems received awards from Academy of American Poets, English Speaking Union, also prizes from the Graduate English Department of City College of New York.

Thanks for faith to Jessie Lendennie, Siobhan Hutson.

Without the scholarship and mentorship of these Women: Mary Jackson, Marilyn Hacker, Charlotte Mandel, Marie Ponsot and Elizabeth Mazzola: my book might not be born, certainly not delivered. Gratitude for close reading, close friends: Eva Oppenheim, Michael Morical, Nicholas Johnson & especially to the generosity of Philip Miller.

(1st, last to JDB & SB, MD)

PATRICIA BRODY's first poetry collection, *American Desire*, was selected by Finishing Line Books for a 2009 New Women's Voices Award. Brody studied writing at Sarah Lawrence College with Grace Paley, and later received an MSW from Columbia and an MA in English from City College. Brody taught American Literature at Boricua College and has practiced as a family therapist for thirty years. Currently, she teaches Seeking Your Voice, a poetry workshop, at Barnard College Center for Research on Women. She and her husband raised three children a block from the Hudson River.